X-traOrdinary X-tremes

Look for other

titles:

X-traOrdinary
X-tremes

by Mary Packard

and the Editors of Ripley Entertainment Inc.

illustrations by Leanne Franson

SCHOLASTIC INC.

New York   Toronto   London   Auckland   Sydney
Mexico City   New Delhi   Hong Kong   Buenos Aires

Developed by Nancy Hall, Inc.
Designed by R studio T
Cover design by Atif Toor
Photo research by Laura Miller

ISBN 0-439-56422-0

12 11 10 9 8 7 6 5 4 3 2 1   3 4 5 6 7 8/0

Printed in the U.S.A.   40
First printing, October 2003

Contents

X-traOrdinary
X-tremes

Introduction

Totally Out There!

For more than 80 years, the Ripley's Believe It or Not! files have been the world's number one source for extremes. Robert Ripley went to all kinds of extremes in his relentless pursuit of the unbelievable. The first millionaire cartoonist in history, Ripley traveled to more than 200 countries and covered 24,000 miles, many of them by donkey, horse, and camel. He found extraordinary people in all walks of life and scattered throughout many countries. When he got home, he couldn't wait to feature these people in his cartoons.

The Ripley archives are filled with accounts of extraordinary people participating in extreme sports or performing awesome feats, each one a thrilling combination of daring and imagination. Included

are such people as Dick Wyatt, who water-skied while balancing on a high stepladder, and Henri Rechatin, who crossed Niagara Falls on a specially-built motorcycle as his wife dangled below, a mere 170 feet from the whirling waters.

Other Believe It or Not! favorites are artists who have gone to extremes to create their art—like Jan Fabre, who creates beautiful murals with the jewel-like wing cases of beetles, or Barney Smith, who uses a most unusual "canvas"—toilet seats. One artist, Evelyn Rosenberg, gets the results she wants by blowing up her work with explosives! Now *that's* extreme!

In this book, you'll meet performance artists who

tattoo every inch of
their bodies or pierce
their skin from head to
toe. And you'll meet
people who go to
extremes to earn a
living, from armpit
sniffers to cave
explorers to fish
stompers.

One of the most famous and fascinating
personalities of the 20th century, Robert Ripley
established a tradition of discovery that the editors of
Ripley Entertainment continue to this day. So get ready
to enter a world of extremes. Test your own extreme I.Q.
with the That's a Stretch! quizzes and Brain Busters in
each chapter. Once you've finished, you'll start noticing
that the world is full of extraordinary extremes—many of
them just waiting to be discovered by you.

Believe It!®

Here are some sports that are probably too daring or too weird to be offered in your school!

Look Ma, No Skis! You need to be pretty coordinated to become a great skiier. But skiing without water skis, boards, or shoes? That's extreme! The United States won the World Barefoot Championship team title six times between 1988 and 1998.

That's a Stretch!

Believe It or Not! In 1897, Manuel Garcia, a Spanish matador, fought a bull . . .

a. while recovering from three broken ribs.
b. while riding an ostrich.
c. with one hand tied behind his back.
d. while riding a bicycle.

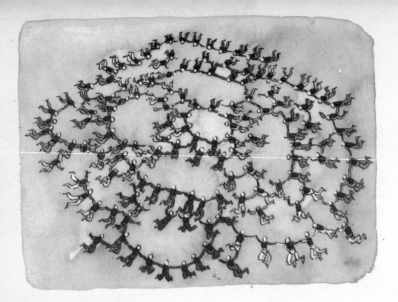

Sticking Together: On December 14, 2002, 300 sky divers jumped from 14 planes and came together to form a circle in the sky above Eloy, Arizona, setting a new world record for the largest free-fall formation.

Dropping By: On August 16, 1960, sky diver Joseph Kittinger jumped from a high-altitude balloon more than 19 miles above New Mexico. In the longest delayed parachute jump ever, Kittinger fell 4.5 minutes at speeds of up to 614 miles per hour before pulling the rip cord to open his parachute and float the remaining 3.4 miles down to Earth!

That's a Stretch!

In 1926, the famous dancer, Billy "Bojangles" Robinson, set the world record for . . .

a. sprinting backward in a 100-meter dash.
b. juggling the most rubber balls while tap dancing.
c. playing the harmonica while standing on his head.
d. tap dancing on a high wire across the Grand Canyon.

Tennis, Anyone?

For Jason Hider and Sally Hathaway, the best tennis court was in the air. One by one, they jumped from a plane and, using basic parachuting  techniques, adjusted their bodies to get ready to play. Then the game began. Playing tennis while in free fall meant that the players had to do a little maneuvering in order to hit the ball. But for these two daredevils, that's what made the game fun.

Pulling Strings:

On October 16, 1988, Eddie Turner  saved the life of fellow parachutist Frank Farnan, who was knocked unconscious after colliding with another sky diver while jumping out of an aircraft at 13,000 feet. Turner pulled Farnan's rip cord at 1,800 feet, over Clewiston, Florida, less than ten seconds before they hit the ground!

Cutting Edge:

As if bungee jumping wasn't risky enough, Ron Jones recently raised the stakes. Instead of wearing a normal bungee cord, Jones leaped from a 200-foot tower wearing a special cutaway cord that he designed himself. With split-second timing, Jones released the cord the moment he touched the ground. This stunt required perfect timing. Releasing the cord too soon or too late could have resulted in injury or even death.

Street Smarts: Before 1995, Tom Mason was a race-car driver, motorcyclist, and wind surfer. But Mason found that none of these sports could equal the rush of racing down a street on his back at more than 80 miles per hour. One of the most dangerous of extreme sports, street luge requires racers to shoot down paved roads on aluminum boards within barely an arm's length of each other. In 1998, Mason set an official world record when he accelerated to a speed of 81.28 miles per hour at Mount Whitney in California.

Board Member: Tony Hawk has taken skateboarding where no one's ever gone before. At age 14, he went pro and was called a prodigy by *Sports Illustrated*. Two of Hawk's most spine-tingling maneuvers are a 900-degree trick in which he spins his body two and a half times in the air while holding on to his board, and the 720-degree varial in which he and his board spin completely around twice and land backward. So far, no one else has been able to duplicate either of these moves!

That's a Stretch!

It was common practice in ancient Greece for contestants in the Olympic Games to compete . . .

a. for prize money.
b. for land.
c. while singing their national anthem.
d. while naked.

Across the Board:

Sandboarding combines the thrills of snowboarding, skateboarding, and surfing in a single sport. To glide gracefully from dune to dune, sandboarders adapt snowboard moves. They master advanced skateboarding techniques to

attack many small hills in a row. And since sand provides roughly the same resistance as water, they use surfing skills to maintain balance and guide their boards. In 1998, sandboarder Nancy Sutton Tenyon was clocked at 44.7 miles per hour, setting a world record for this sport.

. . . Had a Great Fall: In spring 1992, Garret Bartelt went to Alaska to compete in the World Extreme Skiing

Championship. During the competition, he tumbled down the mountain's steepest slope in the longest fall in professional skiing history. Extreme skiers wear no protective gear but—Believe It or Not!—Bartelt's injuries turned out to be minor, and two years later, he was back on the slopes competing in another world championship.

Deep Blue Diva:

Have you ever tried to hold your breath for more than a minute? That's about the longest most of us can manage without training. Mehgan Heaney-Grier can do better than that. She can hold her breath for 5 minutes and 36 seconds. Several years ago, she was sailing with deep-sea diver

friends who dared her to try diving without an oxygen tank. Free diving is risky. One hazard is shallow-water blackout—a phenomenon that causes instant death. Free-diving to a depth of 60 feet is a major challenge, even for someone who's experienced. Unbelievably, Heaney-Grier plunged to a depth of 87 feet on her first try! In 1997, Heaney-Grier dived 165 feet, setting the first free-diving record in the United States. Currently, she's training five hours a day, six days a week, to prepare for her next feat—a 200-foot dive, the equivalent of jumping off a 20-story building.

That's a Stretch!

Parisian Jean-Yves Blondeau invented a suit that makes it possible for him to pursue the new extreme sport of . . .

a. full-body skating.
b. butt boarding.
c. deep-sea skateboarding.
d. street-luge kiteboarding.

Water Table: In 1952, the team of Dick Wyatt and Willa McGuire amazed audiences by using specially modified tabletops to water-ski. McGuire skied while standing on a chair that was precariously balanced on her ski table. Raising the stakes, Wyatt placed a stepladder on his table, climbed to the top, and effortlessly glided across the water.

Toe to Toe: Each year, the World Toe Wrestling Championships are held in England to crown the world's best male and female toe wrestlers. To win, a player has to push an opponent's foot to the other side of a ring, called a toerack, using only his or her toes. Each winner takes away a trophy and a six-month supply of Ben & Jerry's ice cream. Multiple record setters are Karen Davies for the women's title and Alan Nash for the men's.

Paddleboard Champions: In July 1996, seven members of the Southern California Paddleboard Club crossed the English Channel from Dover, England, to Cape Gris-Nez, France, in six hours and 20 minutes. Three years later, they came to New York City hoping to break the record for circling Manhattan Island by paddleboard. On June 11, 1999, they hit the charts by circumnavigating the island in six hours, eight minutes.

That's a Stretch!

In Patzcuaro, Mexico, residents celebrate the New Year by playing a hockeylike game. For a puck, they use a . . .

a. bag of tomatoes.
b. bag filled with firecrackers.
c. ball made of burning rags.
d. ball of cow dung.

Playing for Hay: Rebate may be the star of the Marengo, Ohio, basketball team, but he'll never make it to the NBA. That's because he's a donkey, one of about 80 owned by Jack Spicer. Spicer's father started Buckeye Donkey Basketball in 1934. One challenge for the human players is to get the donkeys moving in the right direction. Another is to stay on the donkeys while throwing the ball. People actually pay money to watch these games, which is why they are such a hit with fund-raisers all across America.

Trunk Show: The ancient sport of elephant polo is being revived in Thailand. Each elephant carries a polo contestant and a trainer who directs the elephant. The main difference between elephant polo and polo played on horseback is speed. Horses gallop at 40 miles per hour, while elephants rarely exceed 15 miles per hour. Then there's the dung. Luckily, if the ball lands in it, a man with a giant-size pooper-scooper is there to clean it up.

On the Fly: Although pigeons have been used for centuries to deliver messages, the sport of pigeon racing wasn't born until the 1800s. The average racing pigeon flies at speeds of 45–50 miles per hour. It is not uncommon for a racing pigeon released at dawn 500 miles from its home to arrive back by nightfall. These pedigreed specimens are bred especially for racing and can cost thousands of dollars. Invincible Spirit, who beat 27,157 other pigeons to win the 1992 Barcelona International Race, was purchased for more than £110,000, or about $160,000, the most money ever paid for a bird.

That's a Stretch!

British equestrian Jonathan James Toogood was known for his strange habit of . . .

a. riding his horse naked through town.
b. straddling two horses at once.
c. jumping hedges while riding his horse backward.
d. riding upside down on his horse.

On Target:

Byron Ferguson is acknowledged as the best archer in the world. How good is he? Imagine shattering an aspirin thrown into the air, spearing a gold ring on the way to the target, or piercing three balloons in a row. Ferguson makes all these shots look easy!

No Bull: Australian cowboy Roger Forster uses his skill with a bullwhip to help him survive in the outback. He

once demonstrated its other uses to a class of schoolchildren, who couldn't help but be impressed when he flicked a golf ball off the head of one student and removed a coin that was on the outstretched tongue of another—without touching either child!

Bull Sessions: Thirty-five hundred years ago, girls on the island of Crete practiced the dangerous sport of bull jumping—grabbing a charging bull by the horns and allowing the enraged animal to toss them onto its back.

Shooting Star: Peashooters of the world, take note: In 1999, 2000, and 2001, teenager David Hollis was the record holder of the most consecutive titles in the World Pea Shooting Championship held in Great Britain. He won with a laser-sighted peashooter he made himself. To play, contestants aim at a dartboard-size target that has been smeared with putty. Five points are earned for hitting the inner ring, three for the middle, and one for the outer circle.

That's a Stretch!

In 1931, at a tournament in Kiev, Ukraine, Wasyl Besbordny and Michalko Goniusz participated for 30 hours in the unlikely sport of . . .

a. knot tying.
b. face slapping.
c. jumping rope.
d. kick the can.

A Real Kick in the Head:

Kickboxing is a popular spectator sport in Thailand. One of its biggest promoters, Yodthong Sriwaralak, has given the sport a new twist—blindfolds for the competitors. During each bout, the blindfolded boxers wear bells so they can find each

other. Unfortunately, the boxers sometimes get confused and end up kicking the referee by mistake!

That's a Stretch!

In the basketball-like game of *tlachtli,* played by the ancient Aztecs in Mexico, every time a player scored, he was allowed to . . .

a. dunk his opponent in a vat of chocolate.

b. grab clothing and jewelry from spectators.

c. throw a pie at the opposing team.

d. jump in a pool to cool off.

Spine-tingling Suspense:

History was made in Toronto, Canada, in November 2002 when Peter Lovering's rock smashed his opponent's scissors in the first International RPS (Rock, Paper, Scissors) championship.

Ripley's Believe It or Not!® Brain Buster

You're on! It's time to test *your* ability to tell fact from fiction and get your very own Ripley's rank!

Robert Ripley dedicated his life to seeking out the bizarre and unusual. But every unbelievable thing he recorded was known to be true. In the Brain Busters at the end of every chapter, you'll play Ripley's role—trying to verify the fantastic facts presented. Each Ripley's Brain Buster contains a group of four shocking statements. But of these so-called "facts," **one** is **fiction**. Will you **Believe It!** or **Not!**?

Wait—there's more! Following the Brain Busters are special bonus games called "Match the Marvel!" where you can earn extra points! Keep score by flipping to the end of the book for the answer key and a scorecard.

Extreme sports are extremely cool! The athletes seem to accomplish the impossible. But all of the sports moments below really happened—except one. Can you pick out the impostor?

a. At the 2002 Gravity Games, Motocross competitors Travis Pastrana and Mike Metzger both landed back flips, making them the first riders ever to complete this X-treme stunt in competition!

Believe It!   **Not!**

b. Reid, Tyler, and Liam Jackson of London, England, are a world renowned trio of brothers specializing in trick snowboarding. The brothers form pyramids and throw coordinated flips and jumps—all on specially designed snowboards.

Believe It! **Not!**

c. Mat Hoffman made history at the 2002 X Games in the Bike Stunt Vert by successfully landing a no-handed 900—that's two and a half flips!

Believe It! **Not!**

d. In 2001, 13-year-old rock climber Tori Allen reached the summit of El Capitan, a sheer granite peak in Yosemite National Park, making her the youngest female in history to complete the 3,000-foot climb.

Believe It! **Not!**

• •

BONUS GAME—Match the Marvel!

Extreme sports are so popular now that it's hard to imagine life without them! Most extreme sports have developed over time, morphing through different forms before becoming the sport you know today. Can you match the early versions of extreme sporting equipment below to the devices they have become?

1. Butt boards   **a.** Snowboards
2. Snurfs   **b.** Skateboards
3. Skurfs   **c.** Wakeboards
4. Sidewalk surfboards **d.** Street luge boards

20

CHAPTER 2

X-treme Daring

Extreme stunts require intensive training and lots of backup in case anything goes wrong. In other words, don't try these stunts at home!

That's a Stretch!

In 1938, Leona Young astounded audiences with her ability to withstand the heat from a blowtorch on her . . .

a. feet.
b. hands.
c. ears.
d. tongue.

Skywalker: On May 4, 1998, while suspended at a height of more than three miles over the town of Marshall, Michigan, sky diver Mike Howard of Great Britain walked on an aluminum bar between two hot-air balloons. There were no harnesses or ropes to ensure his safety. All he had was a pole to help him keep his balance!

One Cool Guy: In December 2000, street magician David Blaine executed his most extreme stunt ever. With doctors standing by to monitor his condition, Blaine spent 62 hours on a street in New York City inside a six-ton block of ice as spectators looked on in amazement.

Big Chill: Yoga master Wim Hof of Holland holds the record for ice diving. His record-breaking stunt took place in northern Finland, where two holes were drilled in the two-foot-thick ice 164 feet apart. The temperature of the water was below freezing, just two degrees warmer than the water suffered by passengers from the *Titanic*. Hof dived through the entrance hole and began to swim, guided by a lighted cord that had been laid on the surface. One minute, six seconds later, Hof's head pushed through the exit hole, setting a new record for ice diving.

Balancing Act: Early in the morning of June 4, 1975, Henri Rechatin, a Frenchman and high-wire performer, came up with a novel way to cross Niagara Falls. It was a challenge that required three people and a motorcycle. Frank Lucas drove the specially-built motorcycle across a cable that spanned Niagara Falls, while Rechatin balanced himself atop it on a metal frame. The last of

the daredevils was Rechatin's wife, Janyck, who hung upside down from another frame attached to the bottom of the motorcycle. Although the trip was successful, the final outcome was not. Police arrested Rechatin and charged him with performing a dangerous act.

That's a Stretch!

In the 1930s, Joe Horowitz of Los Angeles, California, was known as the "Man with the Iron Nose" because he . . .

a. could use his nose as a metal detector.
b. had no sense of smell.
c. was a boxer who never had a broken nose even though he was punched hundreds of times.
d. could balance an 18-pound sword on his nose.

On a Wing and a Prayer: To demonstrate that she was as daring as any man, Lillian Boyer, a stunt flier of the 1920s, hung from the wing of an airborne plane by one hand.

Fire Work: In 1986, Allison Bly, a performance artist who just happened to be an expert in explosives, came up with a stunt that no one else could—or should—hold a candle to. She lies down inside a box with explosives equal to two sticks of dynamite and lights a fuse, setting off an ear-splitting explosion. So far, Bly has survived more than 1,100 explosions inside what she refers to as "The Coffin."

Pushing the Limits:

Escape artist Robert Gallup wanted to attempt the Death Dive—something even the most experienced stunt people would probably back away from. Here's the reason: The stunt involves being dropped out of a plane while handcuffed and

chained inside a mail bag that is locked inside a cage. The catch? Gallup could pick locks, but he didn't know how to sky dive. Luckily, he was a quick study. In just nine months, he achieved his goal and—thankfully— his training paid off. Without a second to spare, Gallup escaped his cage in time to activate his parachute and float safely to the ground.

That's a Stretch!

Harry McGregor could pull his wife, Lillian, in a wagon using only his . . .

a. pinky.
b. teeth.
c. eyelids.
d. toes.

Shell Game:
In the 1920s, Joseph Darby of Dudley, England, could jump on an open basket of eggs and then leap off again with such lightning speed that he would not crack a single shell.

High on Herself: In 1931, a tightrope stretched between two New York City skyscrapers in Times Square was the stage for young Birdie Tillman. With no net or safety mechanisms, Tillman crossed from one building to the other, hanging by her mouth from a metal bar that was attached to the rope. Her unbelievable performance will probably never be duplicated because current New York City laws prohibit such exhibitions.

No Breaks: A contortionist called "The Great Johnson" could balance his entire weight on a single small juice glass.

That's Using His Head!

In 1999, John Evans of Heanor Derbyshire, England, balanced a car on his head for 33 seconds.

Hanging Out: When suspension artist Joey Strange began dreaming about flying over the Hollywood sign in California, he decided to see if he could make his wish come true. How? By having heavy metal hooks embedded in his back and legs and being suspended from a helicopter. Sound painful? The piercing took an hour, and then while a whole team of paramedics waited below, Strange was carried off by the helicopter (*see color insert*). Strange says that soaring 1,000 feet above the Hollywood sign without a net was so exhilarating that he soon forgot about the pain—Believe It or Not!

That's a Stretch!

When she was just 15 years old, Shannon Pole Summer . . .

a. pulled a truck packed with a high school football team.
b. pulled a fire truck.
c. bench-pressed a piano.
d. lifted a compact car to her shoulders.

Getting Rattled: Jackie Bibby knows how to handle snakes. He holds the record for sharing a bathtub with 35 rattlers. He has also received many awards at the National Rattlesnake Sacking Championships held each spring in Taylor, Texas. The object of the contest is to put ten live rattlesnakes into a sack in the shortest time possible. The snakes have not been tamed, defanged, or de-venomed. The rules are harsh—including a five-second penalty each time a contestant gets bitten!

That's a Stretch!

In the 1930s, Dagmarr Rothman was known for this most unusual ability.

a. Swallowing a mouse and bringing it back up unharmed.
b. Eating metal.
c. Walking on hot coals.
d. Blowing up balloons through his eye sockets.

Bugging Out: Dean Sheldon has developed an unusual skill—the ability to hold poisonous scorpions in his mouth without getting hurt. On November 24, 2001, he broke his own record by holding 21 scorpions in his mouth for a total of 18 seconds.

Head Trip:

Gao Fu Zhoa helped usher in the Year of the Snake in a most unusual way. On January 9, 2001, the 50-year-old performer from China fed a 25-inch-long snake through his nostril, down his throat, and out his mouth. Gao performed his stunt at a Singapore shopping center 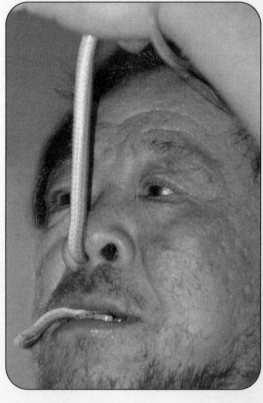 as part of the festivities being held in honor of the Lunar New Year. According to Gao, only two other people have attempted this amazing feat.

All Caught Up:

Magician Criss Angel once spent six hours dangling from a ceiling on fishhooks. In 2002, shackled in chains and wearing a scubalike breathing mechanism, Angel submerged himself upside down for 24 hours in a 220-gallon tank of water in New York City's Times Square.

Up a Wall: Joaquim Hindren is going nowhere but up. On October 20, 2001, in Helsinki, Finland, Hindren set a record by climbing a vertical wall nearly ten feet tall—pretty extreme when you consider that he was on a motorcycle at the time!

That's a Stretch!

Li Jian Hua of China lifted 110 pounds, 1.6 ounces using only . . .

a. one arm.
b. his ears.
c. his teeth.
d. one ankle.

Heavy Hitter: Joseph Ponder of Love Valley, North Carolina, enjoyed smashing cement blocks with a 20-pound sledge hammer moving at 66 miles per hour—which he held with his teeth!

Trial by Fire: Stuntman Gary Edelen has set himself on fire at least 500 times. Prior to attempting each stunt, Edelen always does his homework. First, he calculates how long it would take to walk x amount of feet in burning clothing weighing x amount of pounds. He also factors in wind speed and then experiments with fire-retardant materials. On August 22, 2002, when the conditions were perfect, he put on three layers of fire-retardant clothing smeared with a fire-retardant gel. Then he put on a fourth layer of highly flammable outerwear and set himself on fire. When the heat became unbearable, Edelen fell to the ground—the signal for his assistants to extinguish the flames. When he was back on his feet, Edelen learned that he had been on fire for 2 minutes and 14 seconds—longer than anyone who had ever tried the stunt.

Swallowed Up: Deep in a jungle in Mexico lies an immense pit called the Cave of the Swallows. A hundred thousand birds live in this underground cavern, which is so huge, it could easily hold the Empire State Building. Since the cave walls are so overhung, there is only one way to get to the bottom—by parachute. Jumper Jim Surber endured six seconds of free fall and speeds up to 100 miles per hour as he dropped through the narrow opening and plunged to the cave floor. How did he get out? Through an intricate winch system that lifted him from the depths of the cavern.

That's a Stretch!

In 1987, Paddy Dole of Great Britain completed 4,100 push-ups . . .

a. with a 50-pound weight tied to his back.
b. with one hand tied behind his back.
c. without spilling a drop from the glass of water balanced on his back.
d. with an alligator tied to his back.

Outrageously X-treme! Daredevils from all over the world have been inspired by Niagara Falls. Three of the following stunts were attempted at this natural wonder. But don't *fall* for the one phony!

a. In 1820, high-wire artist Marie Buster was fined for stretching a high wire directly through the giant waterfall. Though Buster intended to walk through the falls on the wire, she was never allowed to.

Believe It!　　　**Not!**

b. Between 1859 and 1861, Jean Blondin crossed the Niagara Falls gorge repeatedly on a 100-foot-long wire stretched 160 feet above the water. Blondin walked the wire in all sorts of ways—on a bicycle, while pushing a wheelbarrow, and even blindfolded.

Believe It!　　　**Not!**

c. In 1902, Annie Taylor was the first person to go over the falls in a barrel. Though a little the worse for wear, Annie survived the rocky trip.

Believe It!　　　**Not!**

d. Peter De Bernardi and Jeffery James Petkovich made the first pair plunge over the falls in 1989.

Believe It!　　　**Not!**

BONUS GAME—Match the Marvel!

Flying in an airplane is pretty common today. But not so long ago, humans couldn't imagine flying with the birds. Can you match up the following key figures in aviation history to the stunt that made them famous?

1. Amelia Earhart

2. John Glenn

3. Orville Wright

4. Svetlana Savitskaya

a. The first person to orbit Earth in space

b. The first woman to fly nonstop across the Atlantic Ocean

c. The first woman to take a space walk

d. The first person to pilot an airplane in a controlled flight

3 X-tremely Creative

For some artists, normal tools of the trade, such as paints, brushes, and canvases, just don't cut it.

Hood Ornaments:

After Tyree Guyton graduated from art school, he decided to transform Heidelburg Street in his hometown of Detroit, Michigan, from a run-down neighborhood to a place of humor and hope. Guyton has turned everything, from discarded vehicles to abandoned houses, into works of art.

That's a Stretch!

When master sculptor Hananuma Masakichi found out he was dying, he created a sculpture of himself to give to his lover, adorning it with . . .

a. his own clothing.
b. his own hair, teeth, and nails.
c. chains of gold jewelry and valuable furs.
d. a pigskin covering to simulate his own flesh.

Bug Art:

Artist Jan Fabre was hired by the Queen of Belgium to redecorate the Hall of Mirrors in the Royal Palace in Brussels. To the queen's astonishment, Fabre chose a most unusual medium. Instead of painting the ceiling, he used the wing cases of Asian jewel beetles to create a mural as well as to cover the main chandelier. Depending on the light, the wing cases glow in shades of emerald green, deep blue, and ocher. Everyone who sees the hall agrees that the effect is quite dazzling and not creepy at all!

Just Ducky:

Ducks, bears, armadillos, you name it! Leo Sewell creates models of them all from plastic and metal garbage found on the streets of Philadelphia.

Chicken Scratchings:

Artist Paul Warhola of Pittsburgh, Pennsylvania, brother of Andy Warhol, had an exhibit of paintings he created using chicken feet as brushes.

Having a Blast: Artist Evelyn Rosenberg of Albuquerque, New Mexico, uses explosives to create finely textured, deeply embossed images in bronze. She lays sheets of bronze metal to which she has glued such objects as leaves, flowers, and doilies over a plaster mold of her own design. Next, she takes the work to an explosives factory where technicians cover it with strips of plastic explosives and string a demolition cord. Then the fuse is lit, everyone runs for cover, and—

POW!—there's a huge explosion. Once all the smoke clears, Rosenberg removes the debris and takes the sculpture back to her studio to clean and polish it. Her works of art are highly prized and sell for up to $200,000 a piece.

That's a Stretch!

A recent U.S. attorney general spent $8,000 to . . .

a. buy bullet-hole art for his office.
b. cover a nude statue of the Goddess of Justice.
c. buy a sculpture made out of hand grenades.
d. have underwear painted on his dog.

Scrap-o-saurus: Jim Garry of Farmingdale, New Jersey, creates detailed dinosaur skeletons out of old car parts.

Making Headlines:

In 2002, to commemorate the 25th anniversary of Elvis Presley's death on August 16, farmer Roger Baker used his tractor to carve out a giant portrait of rock and roll's most famous celebrity on land he owns in Ellenville, New York.

Sand-witchery:

In July 2001, 60 sand sculptors spent two weeks at the Holland Sand Sculpture Park near Almere, Netherlands, building the world's tallest sand castle. Towering 68 feet, 7.2 inches high, the sand castle incorporated scenes from various fairy tales. But its glory will live on only in photographs. The elaborate sand castle was knocked down with a bulldozer a month later.

That's a Stretch!

The sculptures of men on horseback that can be seen in many cities contain a message. A horse with two forelegs raised in the air means that the rider . . .

a. died in battle.
b. led his men to victory.
c. became president of the United States.
d. was wounded in battle.

Well-Heeled:

In 1947, Anthony Cicale of New York City created abstract paintings using only the toe, heel, and ball of his foot.

Memory Work:
From 1862 to 1898, John Warwick (at left in photo) worked at covering the Old Curiosity Shop in Ballarat, Australia, inside and out with thousands of objects, from shells and rocks to dishes and broken glass. Why? Perhaps the inscription he wrote with shells inside a grotto gives us a clue: "Think of the old man."

Shooting the Works: In the 1930s, Ernie and Dot Lind were known for the bullet-hole art they created by shooting at canvases rather than painting them.

Hair Piece: Artist Manuel Andrada of Ecuador painted a microscopic version of *The Last Supper* on a grain of rice using hairs from the back of his hand for paintbrushes.

That's a Stretch!

David Hammons, an artist in Harlem, New York, once sold autographed . . .

a. flower pots.
b. toothpicks.
c. snowballs.
d. birds' nests.

Painting in Tongues:

In the late 1920s, Chinese artist Huang Erh-nan created elaborate paintings on silk by using his tongue instead of a brush.

Pick-tures: Deborah Lacayo of Oregon carves and paints miniature people on the ends of toothpicks.

TP Art: Artist Wu Luo Zhong has found a new use for toilet paper. Zhong was arrested after arriving in America illegally. But even in jail, Zhong's creativity could not be stifled. Since the only materials available to him were toilet paper and glue, he simply mixed them together with water to create beautiful papier-mâché sculptures. So impressive was his art that he was awarded an artist's visa and set free.

Laundromat Art: Slater Barron of Long Beach, California, creates life-size sculptures, murals, and portraits, such as the one at right, out of laundry lint.

Earthwork: In 1970, using more than 6,600 tons of dirt and black basalt, the late Robert Smithson built his Spiral Jetty in the Great Salt Lake. Built when the water level was unusually low, the 1,500-foot-long, 15-foot-wide spiral can be seen only when the lake falls below 4,197 feet. Then it appears above the pink waters of the lake, its salt-encrusted black basalt sparkling in the sun. Why pink? Because of the red pigment in the bacteria and algae that live in the salty water.

That's a Stretch!

Artist Mary Louse Lynch of Dell City, Texas, creates sculptures out of . . .

a. wasps' nests.
b. ice cream.
c. peanut butter.
d. tumbleweeds.

Making a Splash: Argentine dancers Guillermo Alio and Pascal Coquigny created a painting by dancing the tango with paint splashed on the soles of their shoes.

Made to Scale: Harold Dalton, a 19th-century American artist, created detailed works of art that were like no others. His materials consisted of butterfly scales and the skeletons of marine organisms that he glued to glass slides. The tiny masterpieces were no bigger than a postage stamp.

That's a Stretch!

Artist Jamy Verheylewegen of Belgium creates oil paintings while . . .

a. underwater.
b. riding a roller coaster.
c. ice skating.
d. playing a saxophone.

Sketch Art:

When he was just a little boy, George Vlosich figured out how to form curved lines on his Etch A Sketch. Now he creates portraits with an Etch A Sketch, which sell for $3,000

each. Best of all, he's had a chance to meet some of his favorite celebrities by sketching them. So far, he has met Michael Jordan; Sandy and Robert Alomar; Cal Ripkin, Jr.; and President Bill Clinton, to name a few.

Lid Flipper:

Plumber Barney Smith has a private museum with more than 500 works of art created on discarded toilet seats. Just about anything can become material for his one-of-a-kind creations— eyeglasses, pill bottles, marbles, and even beehives.

Burning Passion:

Tadhiko Okawa recreated Da Vinci's *Mona Lisa* and other classic works of art from pieces of strategically burned toast.

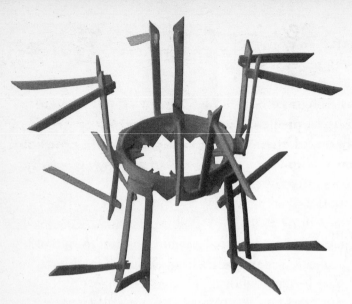

Styrogami: One day in 1982, J. Jules Vitali was so bored at a business meeting that he began whittling away at a Styrofoam coffee cup. The results were quite pleasing. Today, Vitali has created about 1,300 graceful sculptures from Styrofoam cups. He calls his creations Styrogami. Why does he do it? Styrofoam is nearly indestructible, and landfills are loaded with cups people have used once and thrown away. By reusing them to make sculptures, Vitali figures he's making a statement about our "throwaway society"—and keeping some of the Styrofoam cups out of landfills.

That's a Stretch!

Gord Hamilton of Richmond Hill, Ontario, Canada, creates paintings that . . .

a. have hidden electrical elements that act as room heaters.
b. double as televisions.
c. change color according to the temperature.
d. change color depending on the room's decor.

The *Mona Lisa* and *The Starry Night* may be amazing pieces of art, but they certainly aren't as weird and wacky as these Ripley's-style creations! Can you spot the only work of art that is totally created by us?

a. Theodore Waddell of Montana has made art out of roadkill.

   Believe It!   **Not!**

b. Tony Alleyne of Leicestershire, England, transformed his apartment into a detailed model of the *Star Trek* starship *Enterprise.*

   Believe It!   **Not!**

c. Norma Lyon is known for sculpting life-size cows out of butter for the Iowa State Fair.

   Believe It!   **Not!**

d. Jamie Lynn Rocker was an architect at the turn of the 19th century who crafted giant buildings in the shapes of bugs.

   Believe It!   **Not!**

BONUS GAME—Match the Marvel!

It's all in the name—or maybe not. Can you match the following artwork titles to the unusual objects they are made out of?

1. *Nature's Ashtrays*   **a.** A car
2. *Cowasaki*   **b.** Sea shells
3. *Ponti-wreck*   **c.** A motorcycle
4. *Stinky*   **d.** A toilet seat

Some people prefer work that gets them out from behind a desk. You might say that for them, it's business as unusual!

These Fish Aren't Biting: In 1982, after 19 years as a dentist, David Schleser decided to become an aquatic biologist. He's been studying fish—including piranhas— ever since. Piranhas can smell blood from two miles away. They're not very big, but when they're hungry, a group of them can devour a carcass as big as a cow in minutes.

Still, Schleser says the fish aren't quite as bloodthirsty as people think they are. To prove it, he went on TV and swam in a tank of piranhas without getting a single bite— not once, but twice!

That's a Stretch!

In order to be a massage therapist in ancient Japan, you also had to . . .

a. be a weight lifter.
b. have larger-than-normal hands.
c. be totally blind.
d. be unmarried.

Cave Woman:
Louise Hose loves to explore places where no one has ever been before. That's why her job—exploring and mapping caves—is the perfect work for her. Sometimes she has to crawl on her back through tight spaces. Other times, she has to lower herself with a rope to get to the bottom. Being among the first explorers to go through a cave can bring surprises: nice ones, like stalactites made of sparkling minerals, and disgusting ones, like a recent discovery—microscopic creatures living in colonies that hang from the ceiling and drip sulfuric acid. Named "snottites" by an expedition photographer, the creatures survive in poisonous air without light, which may add to scientific research about how life began.

That's a Stretch!

With an annual death rate of one out of every 100 workers, the world's most dangerous occupation is . . .

a. police officer.
b. firefighter.
c. lion tamer.
d. oil rig diver.

Quacking Up:

In January 2003, the Peabody Hotel had a job opening. The requirements? Someone who has a way with people—and ducks! The Peabody, an elegant landmark located in Memphis, Tennessee, was looking for a new handler to lead its resident ducks twice a day on their world-famous march from their rooftop home to

the hotel's fountain in the lobby. Besides the salary, the rewards are great. The duck master gets to meet lots of people and become part of the show.

In the Can: Professional food taster Edwin Rose of Hayes, England, taste-tests cat and dog foods for a living.

Dollars and Scents: Scientists at the University of Illinois are looking for ways to freshen the air around pig farms. Would feeding them different types of food improve the atmosphere? To find out, they paid people to sniff the results. When these people say their job stinks, they're not kidding!

Making Head-way: Cunning Stunts, an extremely imaginative marketing agency in Great Britain, has come up with a new way to advertise their clients' products—using students' foreheads as billboards. They are offering students the equivalent of about $140 per week to wear a transfer made of nontoxic vegetable dye that displays a corporate logo on their forehead for a minimum of three hours a day.

Dragon Breath:

Working as a fire-breather can be hazardous for reasons other than what you might think. When Paul Domenech was stopped for a

routine traffic violation, the officer took one whiff of his breath and charged him with drinking and driving under the influence of alcohol. Luckily, Domenech was able to prove in court that what the officer had smelled was the just the mixture of rubbing alcohol and gasoline that Domenech, a professional fire-breather, had used in his last performance before being stopped!

Holding the Line:

Some people will pay good money so that others will stand in line for them at the cleaners, the department of motor vehicles, or any other place that requires someone to appear in person. This is one job where no skills are required—just a flexible schedule and a whole lot of patience.

That's a Stretch!

Mary Ann Smith of England earned extra money by . . .

a. shooting peas at people's windows to wake them up.

b. rounding up stray livestock that escaped their pens.

c. picking locks for people who had forgotten their keys.

d. making sure that the queen's guards did not fall asleep on the job.

Hot Feet:

Volcanologists spend a lot of time at computers analyzing information. But to get a lot of that information, they have to go out and study volcanos firsthand. This involves taking samples of steaming hot lava and poisonous gases as well as measuring the earth tremors caused by an eruption. Why do they do it? One reason is to learn more about when volcanoes will erupt, so people who live nearby can be evacuated in time.

For Crying Out Loud! Throughout the Seven Years' War against Austria and Russia (1756–1763), by order of

King Frederick the Great, the drummer of the Grenadier Guard Regiment of Prussia was severely whipped whenever a grenadier was killed. This made certain that at least one man would cry for each fallen comrade!

That's a Stretch!

Benito of the Bloody Sword became a pirate because he was . . .

a. a failed politician.
b. a lousy singer.
c. kidnapped and raised by pirates.
d. jilted by his fiancée.

Royal Head Holder: Great Britain's King John (1199–1216) had a servant whose official job was to hold the king's head if he became seasick.

Nosing Around: To determine which products work best, deodorant companies are always on the lookout for people who are willing to sniff the armpits of those wearing—and not wearing—antiperspirants. These workers are telling the literal truth when they say their job is the pits!

Hangman: The fact that Albert J. Smith was a wall-paperhanger in Robert Ripley's office in the Empire State Building in New York City is not so remarkable. But when you take into consideration that he had only one arm, well, that is something else!

Golden Oldie: In 2001, Marta Aurenes was hired as the new bouncer at a pub in Oslo, Norway. To keep fit, she worked out with weights three times a week and enrolled in a police training course for bouncers. Not bad for a 91-year-old grandmother.

Toe Food: In Cambodia, professional fish stompers are paid to stand in baskets, pounding fish with their feet to make a paste called *prahok,* which is exported all over the world. An age-old form of food processing, stomping fish is exhausting work. Those who have never tasted *prahok* may be turned off by its extremely strong aroma, but for many people, it is an unsurpassed delicacy.

That's a Stretch!

In spite of the fact that Willie Boular of Atchison, Kansas, was deaf, mute, and legless, he was able to . . .

a. lay 46,000 paving bricks in less than eight hours.
b. shear 100 sheep in 60 minutes.
c. shoe more than 100,000 horses in a month.
d. make 1,000 pizzas in a single day.

Switch Doctor: In order to resign his profession, a witch doctor in Angola, Africa, must assume an entirely new identity, which he does by wearing a mask day and night for one whole year.

One Leg to Sit On: Here is the strangest safety regulation in industrial history: In Ardeer, Scotland, management at the first British dynamite factory prevented workmen who supervised the machinery from dozing on the job. How? By requiring them to sit on a one-legged stool. It worked! This was the only major dynamite factory in the world that never had a serious accident.

It's Easy Being Green: Jennifer Stewart of New York City makes her living by painting herself green and posing as the Statue of Liberty.

That's a Stretch!

The pay scale for the laborers who built the Brooklyn Bridge between 1869 and 1883 was from $1.75 to $4.00 per . . .

a. day.
b. hour.
c. week.
d. month.

Monster Tracker:
Tod Deery is a director for the Bigfoot Research Project. In addition to field research, his duties include public relations, fund-raising, and educational programming. Job requirements? Expertise in some field of science and a knowledge of anthropology, primatology, or biology. Job candidates must possess a keen curiosity and willingness to be flexible. Oh, yes, they should also have a thick skin: They might have to take a bit of ribbing from people who think Bigfoot is nothing but a legend!

Sweet Deal: In 2002, Fortnum & Mason, one of Britain's fanciest grocery stores, advertised for a chocolate taster at a salary equal to $54,000 a year. To earn his or her pay, a taster must travel the world sampling as much chocolate as possible. It's a tough job, but somebody has to do it!

Squeeze Play: Jesus Rivas and Renee Owens are the world's foremost experts on the giant anaconda. Rivas and Owens take great care recording measurements and attaching radio transmitters to track the creatures' movements in the wild. Because anacondas live in murky rivers covered with water hyacinths, they're not easy to see. So Owens and Rivas rely on their sense of touch and find them with their feet. Among the deadliest creatures on Earth, an anaconda squeezes its prey to death and swallows it whole. These snakes can weigh 400 pounds or more and have been known to attack humans. As many as 110 teeth, which are as sharp as fishhooks, line their vise-like jaws. The more the prey struggles, the tighter the snake's grip. For Rivas and Owens, one lapse in concentration could result in a gruesome death.

That's a Stretch!

Mike Pixley gets about 2,900 rocks a day in his work as a . . .

a. geologist at Duke University in North Carolina.
b. diamond miner in Africa.
c. opal miner in Coober Pedy, Australia.
d. La-Z-Boy chair tester.

Brain Buster

We've got a job for you! Don't worry, it's just another brain buster! See if you can work out the one odd job description below that's made up.

a. A food stylist makes sure that food looks pretty for photographs, movies, etc. Say cheese!
Believe It!   Not!

b. Animal psychologists treat animals that have psychological problems—like a golden retriever with schizophrenia.
Believe It!   Not!

c. A denimologist breaks in people's jeans to achieve the perfect fit.
Believe It!   Not!

d. Mystery shoppers, or secret shoppers, are employed by market research companies to pose as shoppers in order to evaluate different businesses.
Believe It!   Not!

BONUS GAME—Match the Marvel!

An unusual job calls for an unusual name—and below are four of the strangest we've heard. Can you match up each of the following four professions with its correct description?

1. Vermiculturist

2. Demolitionist

3. Riddler

4. Dendrochronologist

a. Someone who destroys things

b. A farmer who raises worms

c. A scientist who studies the history of trees

d. Someone who rotates champagne bottles

When it comes to behavior, people are capable of doing some of the silliest, grossest, and creepiest things!

That's a Stretch!

According to the *Bild Zeitung* newspaper, a couple in Germany were kissing in their car and didn't notice until it was too late that . . .

a. the car was rolling into a lake.
b. the engine had caught fire.
c. a bear had jumped in and was eating their lunch.
d. a tree had fallen on the car.

Worm Chaser:

At the 1990 annual German Oktoberfest in Kitchener, Ontario, Canada, Kevin Roberts shaved his head, covered himself in molasses, and ate a worm—all to win $10,000!

Winning Hand: Shridhar Chillal of Pune, India, has nailed himself a spot in the record books by growing the nails on his left hand to a total length of 20 feet, 2.25 inches. Let's hope Chillal is right-handed!

Spit It Up: Joe "Daddy Eyepopper" Jones of Cleveland, Ohio, can pop his eyes a half-inch out of their sockets, either one at a time or simultaneously. Jones is a weight lifter and discovered his unusual talent while practicing.

X-tremely Gross: If you happened to become ill in Louisiana during the 1800s, several popular "cures" just might have made you sicker! A tea made of cockroaches was a remedy for tetanus, and cockroaches fried in oil and garlic were used to cure indigestion. *Burp!*

From Head to Toenail:

Dr. Kathy Hayes is an anthropologist who studies the unique habits of people all over the world. But now she's the one who's getting all the attention. In fact, she can't go anywhere without people noticing her—all on account of her five-inch-long toenails. Few people have toenails that are strong

enough to grow as long Hayes's. She started it as an experiment in tolerance. Hayes is interested in finding out why people have such a strong reaction to her toenails that they use it as the basis to form opinions about her. Until she finds out, she'll keep the nails long, even if it means that the only shoes she can wear are sandals.

That's a Stretch!

The number of couples who tied the knot at a 1995 wedding in Seoul, South Korea, was . . .

a. 35.
b. 350.
c. 3,500.
d. 35,000.

Crispy Critters: Water beetles and scorpions have long been a staple food of Thailand's northern provinces. Now they're about to become more widely available. Two entrepreneurs, one a former disc jockey and the other an ex-shrimp farmer, have launched a fast-food chain specializing in cooked bugs. Insects Inter offers gutsy eaters a chance to sample a box of crispy fried crickets with chili sauce for the equivalent of just 70 cents. *Yum!*

What a Squirt! Jim Chichon of Milford, Pennsylvania, has remarkable tear ducts that work in two directions rather than one. Because of this rare abnormality, Chichon is able to squirt milk—or any other liquid for that matter—out of his eyes. He first discovered he had this ability when, as a little boy, he held his nose underwater, and bubbles started shooting from his eyes.

Going Buggy:

The students at Iowa State University's Entomology Club really love bugs— especially toasted ones with a little Cajun seasoning.

One club member, Gretchen Schultz, highly recommends crickets in Jell-O. But the recipe all club members agree is the most tempting is the one for chocolate-covered grasshoppers. First, cut off the grasshoppers' legs. Next, simmer butter, brown sugar, and corn syrup to dip the grasshoppers in. Fill candy molds halfway with chocolate, drop in the grasshoppers, and finish filling the molds. Let set—and *bon appétit!*

That's a Stretch!

Every dish in a cook-off at an annual festival in Marshall, Texas, has to be made with at least one . . .

a. fire ant.
b. scorpion.
c. lizard.
d. wasp.

D-eel-icious:

One of the biggest sellers at Fugetsudo, a popular sweet shop in Japan, is sea slug ice cream. If you've tried it and are still hungry, you might like to sample the soft-shelled turtle flavor. In 2003, Matsushita, a Japanese ice-cream distributor, offered its customers eel ice cream. And the next year's offering? A flavor called short-necked clam, which just might give new meaning to the phrase "gross national product"!

Political Wizardry: A candidate for regional governor of Sverdlovsk, Russia, is changing his name in a last-ditch effort to win an election that he has lost several times before. Hoping for a little magical help from a popular boy wizard, he has decided to try running with a different name—Harry Ivanovich Potter. Why "Ivanovich"? Because Russian law requires that anyone changing their name has to adopt a middle name based on the first name of their father.

Weird Weighs: Every year in High Wycombe, England, the mayor and charter trustees are publicly weighed in front of the Guildhall. The sergeant-at-mace calls out each person's weight. If he adds "and some more," the people watching taunt the guilty party because they consider he or she has put on the extra pounds at the public's expense.

Spacey! In March 2003, Dan Foley, a Republican from Roswell, New Mexico, introduced a bill to honor all extraterrestrial beings with a special day that would celebrate past, present, and future extraterrestrial visitors to New Mexico. Extraterrestrial Culture Day would be held the second Thursday in February. Roswell's population doubles each July when thousands of earthly visitors come to this self-proclaimed alien capital of the world—the place where many UFO buffs believe an alien spacecraft crash-landed in 1947.

Feeling Blue: In 1999, Stan Jones, Montana's 2002 Libertarian candidate for the Senate, was worried that chaotic conditions related to the millennium might interfere with antibiotic supplies. So he started taking colloidal silver, which is marketed as an antibacterial agent and immunity booster. An unfortunate side effect? Blue skin!

That's a Stretch!

Former United States senator Barry Goldwater once said . . .

a. "I have opinions of my own—strong opinions—but I don't always agree with them."

b. "When you come to a fork in the road, take it."

c. "I love California. I practically grew up in Phoenix."

d. ". . . peanut butter is darn good shaving cream."

X-tremely Creepy:

The Tlingit tribe of Alaska cremated all their dead except shamans, whom they believed could not burn. Instead, the high priests were embalmed and placed in shelters along with a slave who was sacrificed to serve the shaman in the afterlife.

Heart Trouble:

When he died in 1928, Thomas Hardy's ashes were buried at Westminster Abbey in London, England—but not before the family cat stole his heart. It was later recovered and buried separately in Stinson, England.

All Bottled Up: When a person died in 19th-century Borneo, the body was squeezed into a jar and kept in the house of a relative for a year.

That's a Stretch!

In Europe during the 12th century, certain medicines were made from ground-up . . .

a. monkey skulls.
b. mummy skin and wrappings.
c. crocodile claws.
d. snake tongues.

Body of Evidence: Did you ever wonder how detectives are able to solve a murder even after the victim has been dead for a very long time? It's because they get help from forensic scientists—people who study the processes a corpse goes through as it decays. The more scientists know about the effects of time, weather, and other factors on a corpse, the better able they are to determine when and how someone died. That's why forensic anthropologist Dr. William Bass started the Body Farm at the University of Tennessee. The only forensic lab of its kind, its three acres harbor dead bodies in various states of decay. Some are under leaves, some are in car trunks, and others are in shallow streams or under tarps. Solving murders has become much more scientific as a result of Bass's efforts. Where do they get the corpses? From people who donate their bodies to science. After all, as Bass puts it, "Why should you stop helping people when you die?"

Grave Messages: Donald Mir of Rochester, New York, created a line of greeting cards designed to be sent by the deceased to his or her loved ones after death.

That's a Stretch!

In his will, Bill Johnson of Pasadena, California, asked that his ashes be . . .

a. scattered across his favorite golf course.
b. loaded into fireworks shells and set off in the sky.
c. released into space from a space shuttle.
d. placed in a giant Etch A Sketch.

That's a weird one! Check out these examples of odd-inary behavior and see if you can find the real oddball—the one that's not true!

a. When 89-year-old Margaret Layne died, she left a hefty inheritance, including a $160,000 trust fund—to her cat, Tinker.

Believe It!   **Not!**

b. Charles Osborne had the world's longest case of the hiccups. He hiccupped from 1922 to 1990—nearly 70 years.

Believe It!   **Not!**

c. Robby Fechner was the first man to dive to the bottom of the ocean using a modified hang glider.

Believe It!   **Not!**

d. In May 2003, Kelly Vernon returned a library book—that had been overdue for 94 years.

Believe It!   **Not!**

··

BONUS GAME—Match the Marvel!

The world is filled with all kinds of different cultures and traditions. Since people usually grow up within one culture, foreign customs may seem odd—even unbelievable. Can you match the common customs below to the countries they belong to?

1. It is considered rude to enter someone's house without taking off your shoes.

   a. Thailand

2. In conversation, a person may refer to him or herself by pointing to his or her own nose.

   b. Taiwan

3. At a meal, it is improper to help oneself to cheese more than one time.

   c. United States

4. Once a year, on the first day of April, it is common to play pranks on your friends.

   d. France

POP QUIZ

X-hausted yet? You'd better not be! It's time to test your X-pert knowledge of everything X-treme! The following quiz is a review of all the amazing facts you've read about in this book. And it's worth a ton of points for your brain busters score! X-cellent!

1. Which of these skydiving stories has been pulled out of thin air?
a. When 300 sky divers came together to form a circle in the sky in 2002, they also formed the largest free-fall formation in history.
b. In 2003, brothers Seth and Jason Kaufman played an alternate version of leapfrog during a 10-mile free fall.
c. Joseph Kittinger fell 16 miles before opening his parachute in the longest delayed parachute jump ever.
d. Jason Hider and Sally Hathaway have played tennis while skydiving.

2. Tom Mason was a race-car driver, a motorcyclist, and a windsurfer before taking up this extreme sport.
a. Skydiving
b. Snowboarding
c. Wakeboarding
d. Street luge

3. The World Toe Wrestling Championships are held every year in England.
Believe It!   **Not!**

4. Bull jumping, as practiced 3,500 years ago on the island of Crete, involved . . .
a. pole vaulting over a bull.
b. a girl grabbing a bull by the horns and allowing herself to be thrown onto the bull's back.
c. a bull jumping over a dozen men lying on the ground.
d. bulls leaping over other bulls.

5. In 2000, street magician David Blaine spent 62 hours on a New York City street inside a . . .
a. block of ice.
b. turkey coop.
c. coffin.
d. beehive.

6. Which of the following balancing acts is a little off balance (in fact, it's not even true!)?
a. The Great Johnson could balance his entire weight on a single small juice glass.
b. John Evans balanced a car on his head for two minutes.
c. The husband-wife team of Dave and Allison Cook can balance together on top of two dozen eggs while waterskiing on one set of skis.
d. Balanced on top of a motorcycle that was being driven on a high wire, Henri Rechatin crossed Niagara Falls in 1975. Though Rechatin survived the trip, he was arrested for performing such a dangerous act.

7. The Peabody Hotel in Memphis, Tennessee, employs an official iguana master to lead the hotel's iguanas on a march through the hotel lobby twice a day.
Believe It!   **Not!**

8. Which one of these amazing animal stories is nothing but a tall tale?

a. In 1842, Robin Wasserman rode an African elephant bareback from Egypt to South Africa.

b. Jackie Bibby has shared a bathtub with 35 rattlesnakes.

c. Dean Sheldon can hold poisonous scorpions in his mouth without getting hurt.

d. Gao Fu Zhoa can slip a 25-inch snake through his nostril, down his throat, and out of his mouth.

9. Artist Jan Fabre decorated the Hall of Mirrors in the Royal Palace in Brussels, Belgium, using . . .

a. butterfly wings.

b. seaweed.

c. the wing cases of Asian jewel beetles.

d. pigeon feathers.

10. Sometimes animals and art go together in the strangest ways. We took artistic license with one of the following statements—can you pick out the fake?

a. Sculptor Shiri Ourian carves anatomically correct frogs out of blocks of salt.

b. Leo Sewell creates models of ducks, bears, and other animals out of plastic and metal garbage.

c. When creating his art, Paul Warhola has used chicken feet for paintbrushes.

d. Jim Garry makes dinosaur skeletons out of old car parts.

11. Artist Manuel Andrada painted a microscopic version of *The Last Supper* on a . . .

a. pea.

b. blade of grass.

c. grain of rice.

d. pebble.

12. Which of the following job descriptions is totally unprofessional—because it's about a made-up profession?

a. Deodorant companies employ people to sniff other people's armpits.

b. Every year in New Jersey, an official pumpkin judge gives the seal of approval on all pumpkins that she deems acceptable to be carved into jack-o-lanterns.

c. Edwin Rose is a professional food taster—of dog and cat food.

d. Some people just hate to wait, so they'll pay good money to have other people wait in line for them.

13. Jennifer Stewart of New York makes her living by painting herself . . .

a. blue, like the ocean.

b. green, like the Statue of Liberty.

c. yellow, like a taxi cab.

d. silver, like the Empire State Building.

14. Because of his remarkable tear ducts, Jim Chichon is able to squirt all kinds of liquid out of his eyes.

Believe It! **Not!**

15. Fugetsudo, a popular sweet shop in Japan, and Matsushita, a Japanese ice-cream distributor, have sold all of the following ice-cream flavors except . . .

a. sea slug.

b. soft-shelled turtle.

c. eel.

d. quail.

Answer Key

Chapter 1
X-treme Sports
Page 5:   **d.** while riding a bicycle.
Page 6:   **a.** sprinting backward in a 100-meter dash.
Page 9:   **d.** while naked.
Page 11:   **a.** full-body skating.
Page 13:   **c.** ball made of burning rags.
Page 15:   **c.** jumping hedges while riding his horse backward.
Page 17:   **b.** face slapping.
Page 18:   **b.** grab clothing and jewelry from spectators.
Brain Buster: b is false.
Bonus Game: 1–d; 2–a; 3–c; 4–b

Chapter 2
X-treme Daring
Page 21:   **d.** tongue.
Page 23:   **d.** could balance an 18-pound sword on his nose.
Page 25:   **c.** eyelids.
Page 27:   **a.** pulled a truck packed with a high school football team.
Page 28:   **a.** Swallowing a mouse and bringing it back up unharmed.
Page 30:   **b.** his ears.
Page 32:   **a.** with a 50-pound weight tied to his back.
Brain Buster: a is false.
Bonus Game: 1–b; 2–a; 3–d; 4–c

Chapter 3
X-tremely Creative

Page 35:   **b.** his own hair, teeth, and nails.

Page 37:   **b.** cover a nude statue of the Goddess of Justice.

Page 39:   **a.** died in battle.

Page 41:   **c.** snowballs.

Page 43:   **d.** tumbleweeds.

Page 44:   **a.** underwater.

Page 46:   **a.** have hidden electrical elements that act as room heaters.

Brain Buster: **d** is false.

Bonus Game: 1–b; 2–c; 3–a; 4–d

Chapter 4
X-treme Work

Page 49:   **c.** be totally blind.

Page 50:   **d.** oil rig diver.

Page 53:   **a.** shooting peas at people's windows to wake them up.

Page 54:   **b.** a lousy singer.

Page 57:   **a.** lay 46,000 paving bricks in less than eight hours.

Page 58:   **a.** day.

Page 60:   **d.** La-Z-Boy chair tester.

Brain Buster: **c** is false.

Bonus Game: 1–b; 2–a; 3–d; 4–c

Chapter 5
X-tremely X-treme

Page 63:   **a.** the car was rolling into a lake.

Page 65:   **d.** 35,000.

Page 67:   **a.** fire ant.

Page 69:   **d.** ". . . peanut butter is darn good shaving cream."

Page 70:   **b.** mummy skin and wrappings.

Page 72:   **b.** loaded into fireworks shells and set off in the sky.

Brain Buster: c is false.

Bonus Game: 1–a; 2–b; 3–d; 4–c

Pop Quiz

1.   **b.**
2.   **d.**
3.   **Believe It!**
4.   **b.**
5.   **a.**
6.   **c.**
7.   **Not!**
8.   **a.**
9.   **c.**
10.   **a.**
11.   **c.**
12.   **b.**
13.   **b.**
14.   **Believe It!**
15.   **d.**

What's Your Ripley's Rank?

Ripley's Scorecard

You made it! You've X-plored all kinds of unbelievable X-tremes in the brain-busting activities throughout this book. Now it's time to tally up your answers and get your Ripley's rating. Are you **A Fine X-ample**? Or are you already an **X-treme X-pert**? Add up your scores to find out!

Here's the scoring breakdown. Give yourself:
★ **10 points** for every **That's a Stretch!** you answered correctly;

★ **20 points** for every fiction you spotted in the **Ripley's Brain Busters**;

★ **10 points** every time you solved a complete **Match the Marvel!** (all four matchups!);

★ and **5 points** for every **Pop Quiz** question you got right.

Here's a tally sheet:
Number of **That's a Stretch!**
questions answered correctly: _____ x 10 = _____

Number of **Ripley's Brain Buster**
fictions spotted: _____ x 20 = _____

Number of **Match the Marvel!**
puzzles solved: _____ x 10 = _____

Number of **Pop Quiz** questions
answered correctly: _____ x 5 = _____

Total the right column for your final score: _____

0–100
Not X-actly

Unbelievable X-tremes may not be your bag. You don't
get fired up about thrill seekers or really far-out art.
Maybe you're more mainstream, more middle of the
road. That's cool. There are lots of other Ripley's
subjects to X-plore. Maybe you're the *Weird Science* type.
Or are you an animal lover? Try *Awesome Animals* for a
totally unusual look at our furry friends. Since it's
Ripley's, it's guaranteed to be unbelievable!

101–250
A Fine X-ample

Believe It or Not!, you're getting in the game. You're
developing a keen eye for separating fact and fiction,
and you know where that leads—right to the wonderful
world of Robert Ripley! He loved collecting X-amples
of X-treme behavior like those you've read about here.
And now you're getting the bug, too. Think you're
ready for more?

251–400
X-traordinary Ability

Whoa! You've got some serious fact-finding skills. You
can tell the true artists from the impostors and the
X-treme stunts from the X-tremely absurd. You are
tuned in to all the far-out and amazing things in this
world. And Robert Ripley is proud of you, even if your
friends do think you're a bit out there!

401–575
X-treme X-pert

What's Tony Hawk's middle name? What's the highest tightrope ever crossed? If the answers are rolling right off your tongue, maybe you've spent a little too much time in the world of X-tremes! But then again, the usual is just so boring to you. Why bother with the everyday when you can live among the record breakers, the trendsetters, and the thrill seekers?

Photo Credits

Ripley Entertainment Inc. and the editors of this book wish to thank the following photographers, agents, and other individuals for permission to use and reprint the following photographs in this book. Any photographs included in this book that are not acknowledged below are property of the Ripley Archives. Great effort has been made to obtain permission from the owners of all materials included in this book. Any errors that may have been made are unintentional and will gladly be corrected in future printings if notice is sent to Ripley Entertainment Inc., 5728 Major Boulevard, Orlando, Florida 32819.

Black & White Photos

7 Free-fall Tennis Game/Tony Hathaway

9 Tony Hawk/Grant Brittain

10 Nancy Sutton Tenyon/Courtesy of Lon Beale/*Sandboard* Magazine

14 Elephant Polo/Kamal Kishore/Reuters Pictures Archive

16 Byron Ferguson/Courtesy of Byron Ferguson

22 David Blaine/Peter Kramer/UPI Photo Service

23 Henri Rechatin/Courtesy of Niagara Falls (Ontario) Public Library

25 Robert Gallup/Courtesy Gallup Extreme Productions, Inc.

27 Head Balancer/Printed with Permission from John Evans/www.headbalancer.com

29 Gao Fu Zhoa/The Straights Times/Reuters Pictures Archive

30 Criss Angel/Ezio Petersen/UPI Photo Service

32 Jim Surber/Mark Lichtle/Aerial Extreme/www.AerialExtreme.com

35 Tyree Guyton Artwork/Lester Sloan/Photographer Showcase

36 Jan Fabre Chandelier/Photography by Dirk Pauwels, Gent, Belgium

39 Sand Sculpture/Michael Kooren/Reuters Pictures Archive

43 Earthwork/Spiral Jetty, April 1970/Great Salt Lake, Utah/Black rock, salt crystals, earth, red water (algae)/3.5 x 15 x 1500 feet/Estate of Robert Smithson/Courtesy James Cohan Gallery, New York/Collection: DIA Center for the Arts, New York/Photo by Gianfranco Gorgoni/Art © Estate of Robert Smithson/ Licensed by VAGA, New York, NY

45 George Vlosich Artwork/Courtesy of George Vlosich Sr./ www.gvetchedintime.com

46 Styrogami/Courtesy of J. Jules Vitali

49 Piranha/© Royalty-Free/Corbis

51 Duck Master Daniel Fox with Ducks/Dan Ball/www.danball.com

52 Pig/Digital Vision

54 Volcanologist/© Jeremy Bishop/Photo Researchers, Inc.

57 Fish Stompers/Darren Whiteside/Reuters Pictures Archive

60 Jesus Rivas and Renee Owens/© Ed George

64 Shridhar Chillal/Reuters Pictures Archive

66 Crispy Critters/AFP PHOTO/Pornchai Kittiwongsakul

69 "Alien"/David Ake/Reuters Pictures Archive

71 Dr. William Bass/John Sommers/Reuters Pictures Archive

Color Insert

(1) Board Games/Grant Brittain; Air Play/ Courtesy of Judy Leden and www.airways-airsports.com; Falling for Each Other/Photo by Michael McGowan Courtesy of GoFast 300 Way

(2-3) Death Dive/Courtesy Gallup Extreme Productions, Inc.; Hollywood Sign/Fred Prouser/Reuters Pictures Archive; Head Balancer/ Printed with Permission from John Evans/www.headbalancer.com; Gao Fu Zhoa/The Straights Times/Reuters Pictures Archive

(4-5) It's a Wrap, Background Image/© Wolfgang Volz/www.wolfgangvolz.com; Blow by Blow/© Dale Chihuly/Photo by Terry Rishel; Painting the Town/Lester Sloan/Photographer Showcase; Beetlemania/Photography by Dirk Pauwels, Gent, Belgium; Air Craft/Courtesy Fan Yang

(6-7) Easy to Spot/© MURDOPHOTO.COM; All Stuck-Up/Zooid Pictures Limited; Face Time/© Mark Campbell/www.silentsongs.co.uk; Body Suit/Bob Baxter/Background Image/© Peter D. Smock/Brand X Pictures/PictureQuest

(8) The Dark Side/James A. Pisarowicz; Dino-Mite/© Nancy Rica Schiff, 1999; Quackery/ Dan Ball/www.danball.com

Cover

(Main Image) Head Balancer/Printed with Permission from John Evans/www.headbalancer.com

(Circles) Tony Hawk (Super Stunts)/Atiba Jefferson; Gao Fu Zhoa/The Straights Times/Reuters Pictures Archive

Don't miss these  other exciting *Believe It or Not!*® books . . .

World's Weirdest Critters

Creepy Stuff

Odd-inary People

Amazing Escapes

World's Weirdest Gadgets

Bizarre Bugs

Blasts from the Past

Awesome Animals

Weird Science

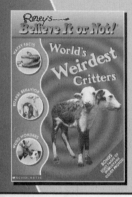